Wiccan Magic

----- ❧❦❧ -----

Wicca For Beginners including Meditation, Magick and Crystal Spells

Lisa Cunningham

© Copyright 2018 by Lisa Cunningham- All rights reserved.

The following book is reproduced below with the goal of providing information that is as accurate and as reliable as possible. Regardless, purchasing this book be consent to the fact that both the publisher and the author of this book are in no way experts on the topics discussed within, and that any recommendations or suggestions made herein are for entertainment purposes only. Professionals should be consulted as needed before undertaking any of the action endorsed herein.

This declaration is deemed fair and valid by both the American Bar Association and the Committee of Publishers Association and is legally binding throughout the United States.

Furthermore, the transmission, duplication or reproduction of any of the following work, including precise information, will be considered an illegal act, irrespective of whether it is done electronically or in print. The legality extends to creating a secondary or tertiary copy of the work or a recorded copy and is only allowed with an expressed written consent of the Publisher. All additional rights are reserved.

The information in the following pages is broadly considered to be a truthful and accurate account of facts, and as such any inattention, use or misuse of the information in question by the reader will render any resulting actions solely under their purview. There are no scenarios in which the publisher or the original author of this work can be in any fashion deemed liable for any hardship or damages that may befall them after undertaking information described herein.

Additionally, the information found on the following pages is intended for informational purposes only and should thus be considered, universal. As befitting its nature, the information presented is without assurance regarding its continued validity or interim quality. Trademarks that mentioned are done without written consent and can in no way be considered an endorsement from the trademark holder.

Your Free Gift

As a way of saying thank you for your purchase, I wanted to offer you a free bonus e-book called **My Little Book Of Wicca Spells**

Download the free ebook here:
https://www.subscribepage.com/wiccaspells

Spells can have a powerful effect on yourself and the surrounds around you. This free ebook has 9 invigorating spells that can help protect your home, bring about luck and help in your careers.

Listen to this book for free

Do you want to be able to listen to this book whenever you want? Maybe whilst driving to work or running errands. It can be difficult nowadays to sit down and listen to a book. So I am really excited to let you know that this book is available in audio format. What's great is you can get this book for FREE as part of a 30-day audible trial. Thereafter if you don't want to stay an Audible member you can cancel, but keep the book.

Benefits of signing up to audible:
- After the trial, you get 1 free audiobook and 2 free audio originals each month
- Can roll over any unused credits
- Choose from over 425,000 + titles
- Listen anywhere with the Audible app and across multiple devices
- Keep your audiobooks forever, even if you cancel your membership

Click below to get started
Audible US - https://tinyurl.com/y2f77sbv
Audible UK - https://tinyurl.com/yyh2c7n7
Audible FR - https://tinyurl.com/y2gskafa
Audible DE - https://tinyurl.com/y44zhcdy

Table of Contents

INTRODUCTION 1
- *What Is Wicca?* *1*
- *Why Wicca Is Beautiful* *2*

CHAPTER 1: WHAT IS WICCA **5**
- *Tenets of Wicca* *5*
- *Is Wicca Different?* *9*
- *What Wicca Is Not* *10*
- *Not Black Magic*...*11*
- *Wiccan Symbols*...*11*
- *Magic Circles*..*13*
- *Law of Threes*...*14*

CHAPTER 2: BECOMING A WICCAN................**15**
- *Getting Started*..*15*
- *Organizational Structure* *16*
- *The Journey* *16*
- *Changing Your Life*...................................*18*
- *Prejudices You May Face*..........................*19*

CHAPTER 3: HISTORY OF WICCAN TRADITIONS ...**21**
- *Gerald Gardner*...*21*
- *Doreen Valiente* *23*
- *Alexandrian Wicca* *23*
- *Algard Wicca* *24*
- *Seax Wicca* *24*
- *Dianic Wicca* *25*

CHAPTER 4: WICCAN DIVINITY **27**
- *The Moon Goddess*.................................... *28*
- *The Horned God*...*29*
- *Dryghtyn*... *30*
- *Phases of the Sacred* *31*
- *Pagan Gods and Goddesses*....................... *31*
- *Fertility and Sex*..*36*
- *Connecting to the Divine* *38*

CHAPTER 5: WICCAN PRACTICES **41**

Animal Guides..*41*
Astral Travel *42*
Candle Magic *43*
Chakras *46*
Crystal Magic..*47*
Divination *52*
Dream Magic *55*
Herbalism..*57*
CHAPTER 6: WICCAN SPELLS 63
Book of Shadows..*63*
How to Create Your Own Spells............................*63*
Different Types of Spells.......................................*65*
Magical Tools... *68*
Spell Descriptions *70*
CONCLUSION 89

Introduction

Congratulations on downloading *Wiccan Magic Wicca For Beginners including Meditation, Magick and Crystal Spells* and thanks for doing so.

Because there is no central authority in Wicca, it is often difficult to know what is and isn't Wicca. This book will present knowledge about the differences between other neopagan religions as well as the tenets, practices, magic, spells, and history of the Wiccan religion.

What Is Wicca?

Wiccan magic is a neopagan religion and a tradition of witchcraft. It is often referred to as the "craft". Wicca is a nature-based religion with roots in ancient practices. In most cases, Wiccan belief revolves around the worship of the Moon Goddess and the Horned God; magic rituals and ceremonies; and practicing witchcraft. Wicca perhaps is best described as a spiritual journey in which the Wiccan practices magic, lives in harmony with nature, and pursues their worship. Some Wiccan even explores their sacred sexuality in rituals and sex magic.

Why Wicca Is Beautiful

Wicca is beautiful because the religion allows the practitioner to explore magical possibilities in their life. By engaging in magical practices, the Wiccan is able to see secrets and mysteries that are invisible or unnoticed by other people. The majesty of magic becomes commonplace for the Wiccan and it fills the world with wonder.

Wicca is also beautiful because it allows the practitioner to live more in harmony with nature. As the Wiccan practices, they become more environmentally friendly, often refusing to use plastics and other non-biodegradable materials. Wiccans believe that nature is beautiful and should be preserved, and so many become activists against the overuse of farmland and the cutting down of forests.

Not only does the Wiccan live in harmony with nature, but they also live in harmony with other people in their communities. As Wiccan ethics revolves around the Wiccan Rede, anger and disagreement become less common and the Wiccan is able to live a healthier life without needless confrontation.

Another beautiful aspect of Wicca is the connection between the practitioner and the divine. Often Wiccans find themselves in closer ties to divinity than they were in previous religions. This is due to the close connection the Goddess and God have with their followers. As one practices magic and worships the Goddess and the God the more fulfilled the practitioner becomes.

Finally, what truly makes Wicca beautiful is the sense of belonging that a Wiccan finds in the craft. Whether or not the practitioner joins a coven, they generally become involved with the Wiccan community, even if it is only by social media. Being part of something greater than their selves makes the Wiccan practitioner more comfortable than ever before. The sense of belonging will fill the Wiccan's life with wonder and opportunity.

There are plenty of books on this subject on the market, thanks again for choosing this one! Every effort was made to ensure it is full of as much useful information as possible, please enjoy!

Chapter 1: What Is Wicca

Tenets of Wicca

There is one law or rule that is almost universally accepted by all Wiccans. It is summed up in the in the Wiccan Rede:

An' Ye Harm None, Do What Ye Will

In modern English this is:

Do what you will, so long as it harms none

Essentially, this creed is the Golden Rule. By choosing not to harm to others, the practitioner does not intentionally hurt other people or make them suffer. Alternately, the line can mean not harming the natural world, which is central to Wiccan beliefs. Ultimately, however, the Rede is up to each practitioner to find a personal interpretation.

There is a longer version of the Rede called the Long Rede. The Long Rede is a 26-line poem with the last line being the shorter Rede. It was first published by Earth Religion News, a neopagan magazine, in 1974.

There are other tenets that some Wiccans practice. Carl "Llewellyn" Weschcke, a prominent publisher of witchcraft, pagan, and occult books presented "Thirteen Principles of Wiccan Belief". According to Controverscial.com, these principles are:

1. We practice rites to attune ourselves with the natural rhythm of life forces marked by the phases of the moon and the seasonal quarters and cross-quarters.
2. We recognize that our intelligence gives us a unique responsibility toward our environment. We seek to live in harmony with nature in ecological balance offering fulfillment to life and consciousness within an evolutionary concept.
3. We acknowledge a depth of power far greater than that apparent to the average person. Because it is far greater than ordinary it is sometimes called 'supernatural', but we see it as lying within that which is naturally potential to all.
4. We conceive of the Creative Power in the universe as manifesting through polarity – as masculine and feminine – and that this same Creative Power lies in all people and functions through the interaction of the masculine and the

feminine. We value neither above the other knowing each to be supportive of the other. We value sex as pleasure as the symbol and embodiment of life, and as one of the sources of energy used in magical practice and religious worship.

5. We recognize both outer worlds and inner, or psychological worlds sometimes known as the Spiritual World, the Collective Unconsciousness, the Inner Planes etc. – and we see in the interaction of these two dimensions the basis for paranormal phenomena and magical exercises. We neglect neither dimension for the other, seeing both as necessary for our fulfillment.

6. We do not recognize any authoritarian hierarchy but do honor those who teach, respect those who share their greater knowledge and wisdom, and acknowledge those who have courageously given of themselves in leadership.

7. We see religion, magick and wisdom in living as being united in the way one views the world and lives within it – a worldview and philosophy of life which we identify as Witchcraft – the Wiccan Way.

8. Calling oneself 'Witch' does not make a Witch – but neither does heredity itself, nor the collecting of titles, degrees, and initiations. A Witch seeks to control the forces within her/him that make life possible in order to live wisely and without harm to others and in harmony with nature.

9. We believe in the affirmation and fulfillment of life in a continuation of evolution and development of consciousness giving meaning to the Universe we know and our personal role within it.

10. Our only animosity towards Christianity, or towards any other religion or philosophy of life, is to the extent that its institutions have claimed to be 'the only way' and have sought to deny freedom to others and to suppress other ways of religious practice and belief.

11. As American Witches, we are not threatened by debates on the history of the craft, the origins of various terms, and the legitimacy of various aspects of different traditions. We are concerned with our present and our future.

12. We do not accept the concept of absolute evil, nor do we worship any

entity known as 'Satan' or 'the Devil' as defined by Christian tradition. We do not seek power through the suffering of others, nor accept that personal benefit can be derived only by denial to another.

13. We believe that we should seek within Nature that which is contributory to our health and well-being.

Is Wicca Different?

The three terms, witchcraft, pagan, and Wiccan, which are often erroneously used synonymously, but there are subtle differences amongst the three.

Pagan is a term that originally was used by Christians to separate Judaism, Islam, and Christianity from non-Abrahamic religions. Paganism can refer to a polytheistic belief in a pantheon of gods, or a monotheistic religion where the Goddess is the centerpiece or even the dualism of Wicca with both female and male parts. Thus, Pagan is a catchall phrase that denotes a large variety of religions, even including Buddhism and Hinduism. Typically, paganism refers to worshipers of a spiritual path that includes a revival of older religious practice and earth-worship. Neopagan refers to newer pagan practices.

Witchcraft is a tradition of practicing magic that dates back to ancient times. Witches are often pagan and/or Wiccan, but there is no requirement for them to be either. Witches can also have a wide variety of religious practices and/or worship different deities.

Wicca, on the other hand, is a form of witchcraft, but it does not follow all the conventions of witchcraft, and it is a pagan religion, but also does not follow all conventions of paganism. Instead, Wicca is an organized religion of witches who follow basic rules and who worship the Goddess and God.

What Wicca Is Not

It is a popular belief among evangelical Christians that Wicca and paganism are devil worship or Satanism. Most likely this is due to the Christians being unable to separate Wicca and paganism from the duality of the Judeo-Christian God and Satan, which are the only two deities acknowledge by Christianity. It is thus difficult for them to differentiate, and so evangelicals usually lump the two groups in with Satanism. Knowing the difference becomes even murkier since the term paganism is derived from a Christian usage.

Not Black Magic

Wiccans are white witches instead of black witches, which are more common in other traditions of witchcraft. Black magic is not used by Wiccans because it goes against the Short Rede and often causes harm or danger to the practitioner or the target of the spell. Wiccans find black magic distasteful, as it does not promote harmony with the earth or spirits.

Black magic centers on the wants or needs of the practitioner without regard for how it might affect other people. Black magic includes necromancy, compulsions, and rituals that involve aggressive, dark, and dangerous malicious spirits such as demons and devils.

Wiccan Symbols

There are many symbols that hold power in Wicca. These include pentagrams, pentacles, magic circles, runes, and other magic glyphs.

A pentacle is a disk-shaped magical object with a five-pointed star within a circle. The pentacle is one of the main symbols of Wicca and is the most associated symbol with the craft. Each point of the star represents the magical element of aether (spirit), air, earth, fire, or water. The pentacle is seen as a white magic symbol. It represents light, love, the elements, the directions, and the divine Goddess and God. The pentacle is used to banish negative emotions and negative energy and is also used to cleanse auras.

While rarely used in Wicca, the pentagram is the reverse of a pentacle. It is also a disk-shaped talisman with a five-pointed star, but the central point is at the bottom and not the top of the circle. The pentagram is popular with Satanists and other witches, however, due to its negative connotations, most Wiccans avoid the symbol. Because of the association with Satanism, the pentagram is seen as an evil glyph. However, its true purpose is to ward off evil spirits.

Runes are another important symbols in Wicca. The most common runes used are the Futhorc, a runic alphabet consisting of 24 letters. German invaders brought the Futhorc to Britain in the fifth century. Runes are typically carved into wood, stone, or bone. These runes are often used as a form of divination. The process for runic divination is to collect the rune stones into a cup or container and then throw them onto the ground. How the runes land determines the outcome of the divination. Runes are also worn as protective amulets and used to empower magic circles.

Magic Circles

Witches often use magic circles in order to cast or practice magic. These circles are designed to protect the Wiccan from summoned creatures, evil spirits, and black magic, as well as general protection from wild magical energies. It can also be used to contain the magical energy that the Wiccan summons while in the circle. Energy gathered in the circle is often created as a cone of power. That is, the base of the energy is from the magic circle, and it rises in a cone shape. The diameter of larger circles can reach up to nine feet. Practitioners can create a magical circle by themselves or in a group. If done with a coven, the circle is much larger and to concentrate the circle's energy and power, the practitioners hold hands. Magical circles are often marked with chalk, cords, sand, or salt. This physical representation indicates the borders of the circle and may be marked with intricate patterns from the Books or Shadows, grimier, or other magical books. In addition to the patterns, names and other magical words are often included in the circle in order to further empower the circle.

Magical circles cannot be crossed without disrupting, dispelling, and or ending the magic circle. This is referred to as "breaking the circle". In order to leave the circle intact, the

Wiccan must open a doorway through the circle with the magical tool that was used to create the circle. This is referred to as "opening the circle". Once the door is cut, the circle may be crossed without dispelling it. However, once the circle is crossed, it must be closed again with the same mystical tool.

Law of Threes

The Law of Threes is a Wiccan belief that whatever the practitioner puts into the world, be it intentions, energy, or magic, returns to the Wiccan three-fold. Hence, if a practitioner puts a white spell in the world that increases love, the Wiccan will receive that love back three times. This is not exclusively for good and white magic; however, it can also be used for black magic and ill intentions. The ill intentions or black magic will also return to the practitioner three times.

Chapter 2: Becoming a Wiccan

Getting Started

The easiest way to get started into Wicca is to find a coven of witches and join them for some hands-on experience. Covens typically include a High Priest or Priestess who can guide the initiate through the wisdom, magic, and rituals involved in the Wiccan lifestyle. Alternately, you can begin with a book like this one or research the religion on the web. However, working with a coven helps to ensure that the initiate is getting the correct information. If a coven is not readily available, the initiate can learn from books like this one or with online resources, however, whenever possible it is best to get hands-on experience with a teacher. The direct transmission of Wiccan wisdom is easier to achieve that way.

In some forms of Wicca, specifically Gardnerian Wicca groups, the coven requires a period of initiation where the novice is introduced to the concepts, traditions, esoteric knowledge, and other practices performed by the coven.

Organizational Structure

It is important to understand the lack of hierarchy in Wicca. There is no central authority in Wicca. Instead, each group has its own hierarchy. Some groups have a definite structure with their own acknowledgment of teachers, books, high priests, and high priestesses. Gardnerian traditions are very structured, while other covens have less organization. This lack of hierarchy prevents the spread of a Wiccan holy book and dogma, with is anathema to Wiccans.

Most Wiccan groups are small and are referred to as covens. The word coven is typically associated with witchcraft in general, but it is applicable to most groups of Wiccans. These small groups gather together to perform magic and rituals, worship and engage in discussions about witchcraft. Most Wiccan covens are around 10-15 practitioners.

The Journey

The first thing to do if you are considering becoming a Wiccan is to read books like this one or websites to decide if Wicca is right for you. Next, learn the various types of magical practices, as well as to gain information about the Goddess and the God. When you have a good base of knowledge, the next step is to think about Wicca. You should consider the concepts of worship, magic, and the practices of Wicca. It is too common for converts to the religion to want to join just to learn magic and never contemplate the Goddess and God worship or the various practices. The basic information about Wicca can be overwhelming with due to an onslaught of information. The convert should contemplate what entering into Wicca means. The convert should also decide if they want to join a coven or become a solo practitioner with no connection to any specific coven or tradition.

Once you have studied and thought about the craft and have a good understanding of the general principles, the next thing to do is to network with other Wiccans. Even if you are planning to be a solo practitioner, meeting other Wiccans can make a large impact on views of the craft. Networking plays an important role in choosing which tradition or coven is right for you if you choose to practice with other people. Meeting fellow Wiccans is also a good way to learn more about the religion, and sitting in on a few coven meetings will introduce you to the intricacy of rituals and ceremonies. If you choose to continue, the coven may wish to initiate you into the group.

The next step is to pray to the Goddess and God, or in some cases the various historical goddess or gods. Many Wiccans choose a patron deity. The Wiccan develops a personal relationship with a specific goddess or god and in turn, that patron blesses the Wiccan and answers her or his prayers. When the Wiccan has a patron, the Wiccan can call upon that deity when practicing the craft or performing rituals and ceremonies.

The final step is to begin practicing the craft. To do so, the convert should have a Book of Shadows or another spellbook with spells, rituals, and ceremonies included. The practitioner should practice the incantations and review the spells before beginning. After you begin casting spells, you are on your way to becoming a full Wiccan.

Changing Your Life

Once you begin practicing the craft, you will see changes in your life. As you follow the Wiccan Rede and use magic to remove negativity you will find greater happiness and confidence. Magic will have a profound impact on your life. As you worship the Goddess and God there will be a deeply personal relationship between the Wiccan and the deity. Many new practitioners have never experienced such a close relationship with a deity, and such a connection adds a new aspect to their lives. This unique relationship can grow, and blossom into a wonderful life experience. Many new practitioners never felt welcome or accepted in other religions. The relationships formed with other Wiccans are the connection those practitioners have sought for years.

Prejudices You May Face

As discussed in Chapter 1, the Wiccan will unavoidably face many prejudices and opposition from those of other faiths, especially evangelical Christians. Members of other faiths do not understand Wicca and incorrectly associate it with devil worship or Satanism. Sometimes no amount of explanation will sway the opposition because they believe that Wicca is evil. No amount of discourse will change the opposition's minds, and it is likely the Wiccan will be persecuted. Also, since most of the population does not believe in magic, the oppositions sees it as nonsense and the Wiccan is often isolated or possibly ridiculed. This especially happens to young Wiccans who are not able to properly defend their faith. With Wicca being a smaller religion and a minority, those faiths currently in power attempt to squash neopaganism and witchcraft traditions. Wiccan must also face adversity at the workplace due to those of other faiths being offended at the Wiccan's religion. In any circumstances, the newly initiated Wiccan must be prepared to face the societal challenges that come along with practicing the craft.

If you're enjoying this book, I would appreciate it if you went to the place of purchase and left a short positive review. Thank you.

Chapter 3: History of Wiccan Traditions

Gerald Gardner

Gerald Brosseau Gardner founded the Wiccan religion. Gardner spent a lifetime studying the occult. Gardner spent time in Asia as a British civil servant. While he is there, Gardner studied Asian mysticism. Gardner claimed to be initiated into a pre-Wiccan coven in 1939. Gardner later started Wicca in 1954, which was practiced in secret due to a British law against witchcraft and because witchcraft was considered Satanism. Even today Wiccans experience prejudice for the incorrect association between Wicca and devil worship, especially from evangelical Christians.

Gardner's practice was influenced by many ancient sources like the Celts, goddesses, traditional witchcraft, and other occult sources such as Aleister Crowley. Gardner's ceremonies were performed nude and were highly ritualized. The ceremonies were intricate and very elaborate. Goddess worship was a priority for Gardner's coven. Members went through initiation ceremonies as they advanced in magical skill and knowledge. Prominent high priestesses in the coven included Doreen Valiente, Eleanor Bone, and Patricia Crowther. Gardner assembled the first Book of Shadows.

Wicca began to gain popularity in the 1960s as it spread across England, the US, and other English speaking nations. The 1960s also saw the rise of other major covens, and new figures in English witchcraft including Sybil Leek, Robert Cochrane, and Alex Sanders. The Witchcraft Research Association was formed in 1964, and it began to print the witchcraft magazine Pentagram. Alex Sanders began Alexandrian Wicca, which was the main rival to Gardnerian Wicca.

The 1970s saw the rise of feminist movements in Wicca, which was referred to as Dianic Wicca. During the 1980s and 90s, there were increased numbers of practitioners in the United States. This is due to there being various witchcraft books, comic books, movies, and TV shows portraying the craft in a positive light. The 1990s also saw the rise of solo practitioners that were not connected to a coven but instead were influenced by the various books of rituals, ceremonies, practices, and spells. The 2000s saw even greater numbers as the books and other resources became available. Today a variety of sources are available online.

Doreen Valiente

Doreen Valiente was a British witch and is often called the Mother of Modern Witchcraft. Valiente first practiced magic as a teen, and later was initiated in Gardner's coven in 1953 by Gardner himself. She went on to become a high priestess in Gardner's Bricket Wood Coven. Valiente proceeded to write several Wiccan texts including the Charge of the Goddess and The Witches Rune. The texts were incorporated into Gardner's Book of Shadows. After a schism between Gardner and Valiente, she left and started her own coven; however, it was short lived. In 1963 she was initiated into the Coven of Atho. The Coven of Atho was an alternate Wiccan coven founded by Raymond Howard. In 1964, she worked with the Clan of Tubal Cain with Robert Cochrane. Valiente wrote several books and many articles on Wicca and the craft. It was Valiente who first suggested that someone does not have to be initiated in order to be Wiccan.

Alexandrian Wicca

Alex Sanders came to prominence in the 1960s. Like Gardner, Sanders was a hereditary witch and was initially taught magic by his mother. According to the historian Ronald Hutton, Sanders was initiated into Gardner's coven. Sanders married Maxine Sanders, and the two became known as the "King and Queen of the Witches". Alexandrian Wicca grew to be a large network of covens and witches. Alexandrian Wicca differs from Gardnerian Wicca because it introduced Judeo-Christian iconography, Qabalah mysticism, and new ceremonies. Sanders was a bi-sexual and opened Wicca up to homosexual men, who previously were excluded because of the emphasis on male and female duality.

Algard Wicca

In 1972, Mary Nesnick founded Algard Wicca. Nesnick was an initiate in both Gardnerian and Alexandrian traditions. Nesnick sought to resolve the differences between the two traditions by merging them into a new tradition. She hoped this would quell arguments between the two groups.

Seax Wicca

Raymond Buckland founded the Seax Wicca tradition when he ceased practicing Gardnerian Wicca. Buckland is noted for bringing Wicca to the United States. Buckland began to reject several concepts of Gardnerian Wicca and in his new tradition introduced Anglo-Saxon influence. Instead of the Moon Goddess and Horned God, Seax Wicca worshiped Woden (Odin) and Freya from

Viking mythology. Unlike the Alexandrian or Gardnerian traditions, Buckland published his rituals, ceremonies, and spells so that they were available to anyone. The book was called The Tree. Seax Wicca also did not require initiation to join the coven.

Dianic Wicca

Zsuzsanna Budapest established Dianic Wicca in 1971. Dianic Wicca was a new fusion of feminist politics and Wiccan practices. Budapest never joined either Alexandrian or Gardnerian covens, instead founded her own Susan B. Anthony Coven Number One. Dianic Wicca was often monotheistic only worshipping the Goddess with no mention of the Horned God at all. Generally, only women were allowed in the covens, and many of the practitioners were lesbians. Unlike Alexandrian or Gardnerian traditions, Budapest published her rituals.

Chapter 4: Wiccan Divinity

Wiccan divinity is pantheistic. The Goddess and the God, who is also referred to as the Moon Goddess and the Horned God, are the major deities. The Moon Goddess is a triple-goddess, and she has three aspects. The Horned God is a dualistic god with two aspects. The Goddess and God are seen as the two forces of the universe. The two cosmic deities are equal. The Goddess and the God have no personified beings like the Judeo-Christian god or the gods of Hinduism, though they can appear in many forms including dreams or using priests or priestesses as mediums. The female and male aspects of the Goddess and the God can be mapped to the five points of the pentacle. Some Wiccans are polytheistic, believing in a host of goddesses and gods, with the Moon Goddess and the Horned God as the ultimate incarnations of these ancient, cosmic figures. In fact, there are Wiccans that go even further and worship the Dryghtyn or Prime Mover and believe that the God and Goddess are just aspects of that even higher being.

Like Buddhism and Hinduism, Wiccans many believe in reincarnation, and that each person is reborn according to their actions in past lives.

The Moon Goddess

The Goddess or the Moon Goddess is a divine figure. She is associated with fertility, the moon, and the stars. She is a three-in-one goddess with three aspects, the Maiden, Mother, and Crone. The Goddess is sometimes seen as more of an archetype with many incarnations from ancient religions and mythologies. These include examples from Babylonian, Canaanite, Greek, and Western Semitic religions. See below for more information on different incarnations of the Goddess and the God.

The three aspects of the three-in-one goddess are the Maiden, Mother, and Crone. Each aspect represents a stage in a woman's life with the Maiden representing youth; the Mother is middle age, and the Crone is an old woman. Each aspect has its own characteristics. The Maiden represents virginity, innocence, fertility, creativity, and youth. The Mother represents nurturing love, caring for children, and growth. Finally, the Crone represents wisdom, age, and experience.

The Goddess is often associated with Mother Earth, and for many Wiccans the two are interchangeable.

The Horned God

The Horned God is the male half of Wiccan divinity. The Horned God is associated with nature, wilderness, sexuality, hunting, and the life cycle. The God is a dualistic god with two aspects, the Holly King and the Oak King. The god is depicted as a creature with an animal's head with antlers or horns and the body of a man. In Celtic mythology, horns and antlers meant that the god represents virility and fertility.

The two aspects of the Horned God are the Holly King and the Oak King. The Holly King rules in the winter and the Oak King rules in the summer. At the Winter Solstice, the Holly King and the Oak King battle and the Holly King are victorious. At Lithia or Midsummer, the two battle again and the Oak King wins.

The Horned God is a god of the underworld, and he spends half a year in Summerland, a Wiccan afterlife. Summerland also called the astral plane is where souls of the dead are kept between incarnations. The Horned God spends the winter in Summerland and the summer in the world of men.

The Horned God is sometimes referred to as Cernunnos, which has Celtic origins. Cernunnos means "horned one". Cernunnos fills all the functions of the Horned God, even down to spending half a year in the underworld. Cernunnos has a connection to snakes. He is often depicted as having snakes for legs or wearing snakes. In one instance, a relief shows Cernunnos is with an unnamed goddess, who is feeding Cernunnos' snakes.

Also from German folklore is the concept of the Wild Hunt, which the Horned God leads. The Wild Hunt is a group of spirits that roam the world hunting the wicked. Seeing the Wild Hunt is an ill omen

Dryghtyn

Many Wiccans believe that the male and female halves of divinity are actually part of a greater supreme being. This being is referred to as Dryghtyn, which is an Old English word for "lord". In Gardnerian Wicca, the Supreme Being is referred to as The Prime Mover, the One, or the All. Gardner held that one cannot really know the Prime Mover and that not only is he unknowable, but the being also has little or no interest in the mortal world.

Phases of the Sacred

Both the Goddess and God are divisible into three aspects. The Goddess has three aspects, the Maiden, the Mother, and the Crone. Some Wiccans also divide the Horned God into three aspects. These aspects are the Youth or Warrior, the Father, and the Sage. The three phases, each represents a stage in a man or woman's life. For instance, both the Mother and the Father represent the middle of a person's life when the person enters parenthood and cares for children. Both have an older aspect, the Crone and the Sage. Each represents age and experience. The Sage is specifically a being of knowledge and wisdom.

Pagan Gods and Goddesses

There are many examples of the Goddess and God pairs in ancient religions, mythology, and folklore. These deities often stand in for the more abstract representation of the divine. In mythology and ancient religions, these pairs of gods and goddesses, who are generally consorts of each other, often take on divine roles while interacting with pagans. For example, Ishtar is the Mesopotamian goddess of fertility and war, and her consort is Tammuz. Many Wiccans have a patron deity, which is a deity who is special to the practitioner and has a close connection with her or him. Patron gods and goddesses offer protection and blessings to those who worship them.

Below is a collection of historical goddesses and gods that Wiccans might worship.

- Inanna and Dumuzi

Inanna, also known as the queen of heaven, is the Sumerian goddess of fertility and war. She is the most prominent goddess in the Sumerian pantheon and is the archetype for all nature and fertility goddesses throughout history. Inanna's original symbol was a bundle of reeds tied into three sections with streamers. It later changed to a star or a rose.

Inanna's consort was Dumuzi, a vegetable and shepherd god, who dies each winter and rises in the summer. In fact, he is the first in a long line of "dying and rising" gods. Dumuzi was charged by Inanna to enter the underworld for half the year.

- Ishtar and Tammuz

Ishtar, also known as Ištar, is the Mesopotamian version of Inanna. Ishtar's symbol is an eight-pointed star. She is depicted as having wings and weapon cases on her back. Ishtar is also a fertility and war goddess. She even carries a weapon that is a part sword and part mace. Ishtar is the most prominent of the Near Eastern goddess, and she has entered popular culture in comic books and other literature. Ishtar spread across the ancient world. She was also worshipped in Egypt where she was regarded as a healing goddess. Ishtar's temples were peopled by high priestesses and temple prostitutes.

Ishtar also has a vegetable god consort, but in the Mesopotamian version, his name is Tammuz. Tammuz is also a god of the underworld.

- Astarte and Baal

Astarte, also known as Aštoreth, is a goddess of sexual love and a fertility goddess. She also represents war and the evening star. She is very similar to both Inanna and Ishtar, and scholars suspect she is in Ishtar's lineage. Astarte is often associated with the Greek goddess Aphrodite.

Baal is the consort of Astarte and the chief god of the Canaanite religion. He was originally a rain and storm god, but he later evolved into a fertility of nature and vegetable god. Baal is also a god of disorder, and each year he enters the underworld. While there he fights the forces of chaos. During the New Year festival,

Baal is celebrated as victorious and he rises from the underworld. Baal was worshipped in Egyptian, where he had a large cult, and Greco-Roman times.

- Ceres and Jupiter

Ceres is the Roman mother goddess. Unlike previous pairs of goddesses and gods, it is Ceres who is the goddess of vegetation instead of the male counterpart. According to mythology, Ceres has a daughter Kore, who is abducted by Pluto and spends half the year in the underworld. In this way, Ceres is associated with the previous goddesses of Inanna, Ishtar, and Astarte while preserving the "rising and falling" aspect that previously was associated with the masculine figure.

Ceres is one of the consorts of Jupiter, the father of the Roman gods. Jupiter was a god of light and oaths. Unlike Baal, Dumuzi, and Tammuz, Jupiter is not a vegetation god, nor is he associated with traveling to the underworld. In the case of Ceres and Jupiter, most of the motifs of the previous are centered on Ceres and her daughter Kore. In this case, little attention is given to Jupiter.

- The Morrigan and Dagda

The Morrigan is a three-in-one goddess of vegetation, fertility, and war. She has the title Queen of Demons. Like the Moon Goddess, the Morrigan has three separate aspects. They are Morrigan, Nemain, and Badb Catha. Morrigan is primarily being associated with nature and fertility, while Nemain and Badb represent more warlike qualities. Nemain represents panic, while Babd Catha is associated with war. Badb Catha's title is Queen of Ravens. Morrigan takes the form of either a young girl or an old hag. Morrigan mates with her consort Dagda in order to bring prosperity. This occurs once a year on the Celtic holy day of Samain. The modern-day holiday Halloween is based on Samain.

Morrigan's consort is the Irish god Dagda. Dagda is the father of the tribe and chief god of the Irish version of Celtic religion. While Dagda is not associated with a specific role, Dagda possesses a mystic cauldron called the Cauldron of Abundance, which has the properties of rejuvenation and wisdom. Like the previous historical gods, Dagda has a ritualized relationship with Morrigan that culminates in a sexual union.

- Eostre

Eostre is an Anglo-Saxon fertility goddess. She is representative of spring. Unlike the other historical goddesses, it is unknown if Eostre had a specific consort. She was worshipped in the spring when young women and girls danced around maypoles. The young women danced in a circle around the pole and each wore or carried a piece of cloth that connected her to the pole. As the women danced, men would come forward and choose a woman to copulate with. The word Easter has its root in the name of the Old English goddess' name.

Fertility and Sex

Fertility is not just a common theme among the various historical goddesses and gods, but it is central to Wiccan belief itself. Fertility does not just mean sexual virility, but also birth, growth, death, and regrowth in nature. For example, a flower begins as a seed, sprouts and grows, becomes fertile and produces seeds or pollen, and dies only to be reborn from another seed. Just as the Goddess and God come in an equal pair that empowers one another, so too comes sexual power in the form of a union between female and male practitioners. Many Wiccans carry on the practice of using sex and sex magic for spiritual empowerment and supernatural energy. Sexual intercourse unlocks many magical powers and provides a wealth of power that is otherwise unobtainable except through sexual climax.

Since sex is not seen as sinful by the Wiccan, but as a natural aspect of humanity, shame is not associated with sexual activity. Thus, Wiccans tend to be freer about sex, and do not dwell on being married in order to engage in sexual activity. Nudity is also sacred to the Wiccan. It represents the original state of mankind before civilization. Most Wiccans are not concerned with sexual preference, and many are pansexual, loving anyone they are attracted to, be it man or woman. However, just because Wiccan's are freer about sex does not mean that any specific practitioner welcomes any sex act, and it should not be assumed that just because someone is Wiccan that they want to have sex with another practitioner. Wiccans are free to keep sexual boundaries and are not required to participate in any magical sexual activity.

The major Wiccan tools are associated with gender and sexuality. A knife, sword, staff, and wand are phallic; while the cup and pentacle are feminine objects and represent the vagina.

Unlike Christianity and other many other major religions, Wiccans do not see sex as a sinful. The druids of the Celtic religion practiced sex magic, where intercourse released supernatural energy that was directed into a person or event to bring a good outcome, strength, or increased warlike characteristics. Sex magic was performed in stone circles or in the druids' sacred groves.

Connecting to the Divine

There are many ways to connect to the divine, be it the Goddess and the God, historical deities or even Dryghtyn. Perhaps the easiest way to connect to the supernatural entities is to pray. Wiccans pray in the same way as other religions. They practice prayer either alone or during a coven meeting. Another way to connect to the divine is by performing ceremonies directed at summoning the Wiccan deities and accepting them into your life. High priests and priestesses and which sometimes require sex magic often lead these rituals.

Another way to connect to the divine is to meditate. Meditation clears and focuses the mind so that the practitioner is ready for the divine presence of the Goddess and the God. Meditation not only clears the mind; it helps rid the body of negativity so that the Goddess and God have an easier time interacting with the practitioner. Once connected to the Goddess and the God, a meditative state helps ensure a successful connection with the higher power.

Finally, the practitioner can communicate with the divine by constructing a shrine or altar. Shrines and altars do not have to be large, and they are a place for the practitioner to put cleansed and consecrated items. A Wiccan might keep her magical tools on the shrine so that they are always close to the divine when not in use. Statues of gods and goddesses often adorn Wiccan shrines, as well as incense, cups, and candles. If the Wiccan has a patron deity, that is the god or goddess that should adorn her or his shrine or altar. The truly important thing is to place items special to the practitioner on the shrine.

If you're enjoying this book, I would appreciate it if you went to the place of purchase and left a short positive review. Thank you

Chapter 5: Wiccan Practices

Animal Guides

Animal guides are a very generic term for several concepts including totems, spirit guides, companions, and familiars. Totems are animals that guide you in your practice. This could be a bird that appears and sings while the practitioner is conducting a ceremony or a creature that appears and literally guides the Wiccan by allowing the witch to follow it. Spirit guides, on the other hand, are the spirits of animals that guide the Wiccan in magical practice or guide them in their lives. Spirit guides can take the form of mythical creatures such as shedu, sphinxes, and dragons. Spirit guides can also be mundane animals such as boars, ravens, or bulls. Shedu is a rarer mythic creature. They are winged bulls from Sumerian mythology. There are statues of winged bulls found in the Sumerian area in the Louvre. Companion animals are animals that are involved in your life and assist in magical practices. Often companion animals add their own psychic energy into the practitioner's spells. The difference between companion animals and totems is that companion animals already have a place in your life, whereas totems approach the practitioner without pre-planning. Finally, familiars are animals that have a magical connection with the Wiccan. Some Wiccans can even see through the animal's eyes and other senses. Not only do familiars fuel a Wiccan's magic, but the connection with a familiar also is usually permanent, and stays until either the Wiccan or the familiar is dead.

Astral Travel

The astral plane is another dimension or plane of existence. It is a place of the mind and spirits where fantastical things can happen. It is populated with many spirits, ghosts, and other celestial or hellish creatures. Astral travel or astral projection is when the witch uses a spell to separate her body from her spirit, which allows the spirit to enter the astral plane or move invisibly throughout the mortal world. Astral travel allows the witch to perceive things usually hidden from her. Generally, in order to astral travel, the witch must be in a trance or meditative state, often appearing to be asleep. Astral travel is done individually or in ritual ceremonies. To perform an astral travel spell, light blue candles in the bedroom. The witch should either lie on the bed or sit in a chair, whichever is more comfortable. Once the incantation is done, the witch should close her eyes to enter the trace-state. Once in this state, the body and the mind will separate, and the mind will be free to roam. Astral travelers are connected to their bodies by a thin white cord or string. If the cord is cut, the connection between the witch and her body is severed, and the witch may become trapped on the astral plane.

Candle Magic

Candles are often used in spells, ceremonies, and rituals. Candle magic is a form of sympathetic magic (see Chapter 6). Candles are used not only to light ritual spaces, but they are also used as symbols of the elements, sources of sacred flames, and positions of focus. For instance, when constructing a magical circle, candles are often set at the five points of the pentagram. These candles not only represent the elements, but also the male, female, and universal points of the pentagram, combining sexual energy even if sex magic is not performed.

Different colors of candles have different meanings in spells. For instance, a red candle is used for passion and love spells, while a green candle is used for prosperity and money spells.

Any candle can be used, though many witches buy homemade candles from other witches. Beeswax candles are often preferred as many Wiccans find they are more powerful. Regardless of where the candle came from, it must be consecrated or cleansed before use. Cleansing them removes negative energy from the candles. If the candle is not consecrated in a ritual, the negative energy it possesses may cause the spell to not function properly, possibly giving a different outcome than what the Wiccan desires.

Incense is important to candle magic. The scents from the incense and the smoke call forth the elements and gather the energy from the practitioner and the radiant energy of nature. Incense often helps the practitioner to concentrate their energy to remove negativity and ill.

Not only should the candles be consecrated, but they should also be dressed. Dressing a candle means putting essential oils on it to seal the magic inside the candle. The practitioner can use any kind of oil, though certain spells may dictate what type of oil to be used. The Wiccan should start with the middle of the candle and work out to both sides.

To prepare a candle for use, the practitioner should start by taking a bath. The practitioner should anoint the bath with salt, then light some consecrated or cleansed candles and light some incense. While in the bath, the practitioner should relax and let their worries of the day fade away into the water. Using meditation the practitioner should remove negativity from their mind. After the bath, the practitioner should consecrate the candle in a ritual. Once the candle is consecrated it should be dressed with oil, and finally inscribed with the practitioner's athame, a ritual knife or dagger.

In order to draw energy or a spirit to you, write on the candle from the top to the middle, then from the bottom to the top. In order to cast off negativity or a summoned creature, write from the middle of the candle to the middle to each end.

Wiccans should be careful when practicing with an open flame. Wiccans should never use candles inflammable places like near curtains, and should also be in a fireproof dish to make sure they do not melt onto the surface they are on.

Chakras

According to ancient Hinduism, chakras, often represented as lotus flowers, are centers of mystical energy found in the body. Nadis are channels or lines of prana (life force) that run throughout the body. Chakras are found along these nadis paths. There are several chakras, each with its own purpose. When the practitioner is using clairvoyance to see auras, the chakras appear as disks of glowing colors.

- The crown chakra is located atop the head. It is the seventh chakra, and it is tied to enlightenment and astral projection. The crown chakra can appear white, lavender, or violet.
- The root chakra is located at the base of the spine. The chakra is associated with the element of earth. It represents the psychic smell sense. The root chakra is red, and the practitioner can chant "ohm" while concentration on the chakra.
- The heart chakra is located above the heart. It is tied to the element of air and mediates the sense of psychic touch. To concentrate on the heart chakra, "ah" should be chanted. The heart chakra appears pink or green.

- The sexual chakra is located above the genitals. It is connected to the element of water and the sense of psychic taste. "Ohm" should be chanted when concentrating on the sexual chakra. The sexual chakra appears as orange.
- The solar plexus chakra is above the navel. It corresponds to fire and psychic sight. When concentrating on it "ah" should be chanted. The solar plexus is useful for clairvoyance. The solar plexus appears as yellow.
- The third eye chakra is located just above the eyes and eyebrows. The third eye is associated with psychic powers. When concentrating on the third eye the Wiccan should chant "eem". The chakra appears indigo.
- The throat chakra is located in the thyroid at the base of the throat. The throat chakra is associated with clairaudience or psychic hearing. When concentrating on the throat chakra "ehm" should be chanted. The throat chakra appears as typically as a light shade of blue.

Crystal Magic

Since the beginning of human history, witches, druids, and holy men have known that crystals and gemstones have magical properties. The specific properties are based on the type of gemstone and the rituals the crystal is used in. Crystal magic is more or less an umbrella term for any type of stone, crystal, or mineral, regardless of the stone's actual composition. Thus, the crystal is a catchall phrase for a wide variety of magical stones. These stones range from agate to obsidian and even diamonds. True crystal balls are made of clear quartz. Below is a partial list of stones and their known magical properties:

- Agate

Agates are stones of the mind and are associated with earth. Agates are generally found with bands across the brown or goldstone. These stones are good for discovering the truth, helping with healing, depression, memories, and improving mental health. Carrying or placing agates under your pillow when you sleep are great ways to unlock the stone's power. Agates are also good for warding off bitterness and reducing anger.

- Bloodstone

A bloodstone is related to the fire. Also known as a heliotrope, the stone is associated with the mystical powers of healing, fertility, and prosperity. The prosperity aspect not only increases positive energy around any project, it especially helps with financial matters. The bloodstone is, as its name indicates, tied to blood, no matter if it is menstrual blood or an injury that needs healing. To help with conception, the bloodstone should be placed under the bed or pillow before intercourse. For financial prosperity, practitioners should carry a small stone in their wallet or purse.

- Diamond

Diamonds are typically a clear crystal, though they can be streaked with yellow. Diamonds are related to both air and fire. While diamonds are typically used for engagements and marriage, it also has other uses. Diamonds are useful for fertility problems and sexual dysfunction, as well as astral travel, meditation, and scrying. Diamonds also increases creativity and helps cleanse auras.

- Jade

Jade is a green stone that is connected to the element of earth. The green stones are known for serenity, true love, and truthfulness. Jade was favored by the Mesoamerican cultures of the Aztecs, Incas, and Mayans. Jade is often worn in earrings or as bracelets and has the property of tranquility when worn. Jade also assists with understanding and remembering dreams, increases confidence, and helps with gaining riches.

- Lapis Lazuli

Lapis Lazuli is a blue stone associated with water. It is good for expanding consciousness, promoting tranquility, and entering other realms and worlds, including the astral plane or the world of faeries. Lapis Lazuli was often used in Egyptian burials to help the dead cross into the underworld.

- Moonstone

Moonstones are white stones that are associated with the moon and the Goddess, specifically three-in-one goddesses like the Morrigan. The stone is good for childbirth, female reproduction, and menstrual cycles. It is also good for intuition and ceremonies dedicated to the Goddess.

- Obsidian

Obsidian is not a crystal but a volcanic rock. Obsidian looks like a black glass, and it is associated with fire. Obsidian is useful for magical protection, clarity, and healing. Like Jade, obsidian was a sacred Mesoamerican stone. Different compositions of obsidian might have other properties.

- Quartz

Quartz is a very powerful type of stone. Quartz comes in several different colors, such as clear, rose, and blue quartz, and each color has its own magical powers.

Clear quartz is connected to all of the elements and is good for clarity of mind, creating and using a speculum for divination, removing negative energy, and unlocks mental powers.

Rose quartz helps bring harmony, enhance feelings of happiness and love, and it emits calming energy. It is also useful for releasing imagination and creativity.

Smoke quartz helps with astral travel, protection, and removing negative emotions.

- Sapphire

Sapphires are typically blue stones, but can also appear in yellow or white. They are strongly connected to both the throat chakra and the element of water. Sapphires are good for treating breathing problems and help with sleep apnea. Sapphires are useful for divination and for connecting with spirit guides.

- Turquoise

Turquoise is a blue stone, sometimes speckled with white or black. Turquoise is useful for broken bones, eyes ailments, and digestive problems. Turquoise is associated with the element of water and is often used in rituals for intuition or wisdom. Native Americans often used turquoise in jewelry.

Divination

The art of divination, also called scrying, is the magical ability to look into the future to see an outcome. Divination is such a common practice in witchcraft that it is essential to know how to scry. There are many ways a practitioner can attempt divinations ranging from dream interpretation, looking into a crystal ball, casting runes, and tarot card reading. Regardless of the specific method, all versions of divination deal with the future and the unseen.

When scrying, it is often important to have a speculum. A speculum is an object like a crystal ball, a mirror, a bowl of water or ink, a flame, and another object that you concentrate your psychic energy on. The speculum acts as a focus and conduit for the energy, which helps clarify the oracular vision.

Divination plays an important role in the history of witchcraft and magic. The use of divination goes back to the beginning of human civilization and beyond into prehistory. There were oracles and seers before humans learned agriculture and began to settle in cities. Recorded tales of divination date back to ancient Sumerian and Babylonian times. Archeologists have uncovered clay tablets that date to between 2340 and 2200 BC. The tablets include a text called An Old Babylonian Oracle, which depicts a seer using divination.

Tarot Cards

One of the easiest ways to divining is through tarot card readings. Tarot cards come in a set of 78 cards. There are 22 cards called the Major Arcana. The Major Arcana are cards that do not have a suit, and each one represents a magical figure such as the Fool, The Hierophant, and the Lovers. The rest of the set is 56 cards divided into four suits. The suits are cups, pentacles, swords, and wands, and each suit has 14 cards.

Tarot readings are done a few different ways. The primary way is called a Celtic cross. The cross has 10 cards laid out. There is one center card, crossed by another card and surrounded by four cards, one on each side. The remaining four cards are placed to the right of the rest of the cross. Another method of tarot card reading involves only three cards that are set out in a row. The cards are drawn face down, and each is revealed in the order of the method for the reading, be it a Celtic cross or another method. Each card is then revealed in order. Not only do the tarot cards themselves have meaning, but the position they are in also has meaning, as well as if the card is upside down or not. An upside down card is called "reversed." Optimally, the person receiving the reading picks the ten (or three) cards from the deck.

Tarot decks are famous for having a Death card. The Death card is a Major Arcana and does not simply mean a death of a person or entity, but also represents a time of change.

Rune Stones

Another form of divination is throwing runes. Runes are carved into wood, stone, or bone. The basics of this form of divination are that the practitioner collects the runes into a cup or other container and then throws the runes onto a table or the ground. Like tarot cards, the position of the rune carries meaning as well as if the rune is upside down or not.

Mirrors, Crystal Balls, and Flames

Mirror divinations work differently than tarot card or runes. With mirror divination, the practitioner looks into a mirror when they cast their divination spell. Visions of the future form in the mirror for the practitioner to see and interpret. Mirror divinations are so common in folklore that they survive today in Disney films like Snow White.

Crystal Balls are another type of divination. Like mirror divinations, the practitioner gazes into the crystal ball as a vision or image form in the crystal ball. This oracular vision imparts secrets of the future. Crystal balls are often sought out forms of speculums for their ability to concentrate psychic energy.

Flame divination works much like a crystal ball or mirror divinations. The flame acts as a focus for the magical energy. Gazing into the flame, the practitioner sees a vision of the future. This is performed with any kind of flame, from a candle flame to a fire in a fireplace.

Dream Magic

Dream magic is very important to the Wiccan practitioner. Dreams are often visionary or prophetic, revealing the hidden, the unseen, and the future. It is also possible for astral travel while dreaming. Dream magic is useful for revealing secrets and hidden things. It reveals when someone lies to the Wiccan and other powerful secrets. It also allows the Wiccan to interact directly with the divine, no matter which Goddess or God the practitioner worships.

To facilitate dream magic, place herbs and crystals around the bed. It is useful to perform a ritual before sleep to ensure the effectiveness of the dream magic. If candles are used in the ritual, they should be extinguished before sleep unless there is someone else to monitor and protect the dreamer. Ghosts and other evil spirits sometimes haunt dreams. A piece of willow in a dream pillow helps provide protection against such monsters. Occasionally black witches will attack the Wiccan while they sleep. Crystals are useful for preventing such attacks.

Another practice that helps facilitate dream magic is the dream pillow. A dream pillow is a consecrated pillow that has herbs placed inside it with spells cast upon it to help improve dreams and the associated magic. A Wiccan can purchase a dream pillow but making their own is preferable.

Herbalism

Throughout history, witches have studied and healed people with herbs. Plants have powerful mystic energy, and using herbs can unlock new powers for the practitioner. There are many herbs with various functions. Liquid herbal remedies are typically made in a cauldron or a cup of boiling water. Herbs can be are bundled together like a smudge stick, or crushed into a powder or paste. Once the potion or herbal remedy is ready, it can be ingested, rubbed on the skin, burnt, put into a bath, or made into tea. The method of use depends on the herbs used and the desired results. Below is a partial list of herbs and their magical uses:

- Aloe

Aloe is used for protection spells and prosperity. It is also very powerful for attractiveness and beauty magic.

- Apple

Apples are typically used in sleep and love spells. The spell is typically cast on the apple and then it is given to the target of the spell.

- Basil

Basil has several magical properties such as increasing wealth, love, and fertility. It is also good for preventing a significant other from cheating and protection.

- Clover

Clover is useful for good luck, healing mental illness, and rejuvenated youth and beauty. Clover is often used in ritual baths. Clover is often considered being connected to three-in-one goddesses like the Morrigan. Four-leaf clovers are especially powerful luck charms.

- Eucalyptus

Eucalyptus is associated with both water and the moon. It is good for relieving worries, mental fatigue, and regrets. Eucalyptus is a protective herb, but unlike other herbs, the protection is short-lived and does not involve attacking any magical energy. Eucalyptus is perfect for consecrating magical tools. Take Eucalyptus in oil form and rub it on the tool to remove negative energy.

- Fern

Fern leaves are a powerful tool in home protection spells. Fern leaves help keep away intruders and prevent evil from gaining entry into the home. Fern leaves can be crushed and spread across the windows in each room. It can also be sprinkled at the front door and then swept out. This creates a powerful magical barrier against evil.

- Ginseng

Ginseng is good for love, healing, protection, and lust. It can be carried in a mojo bag to draw in positive vibes for money, health, and sexual potency. Ginseng is also a powerful herb for increasing desire and wishes.

- Holly

Holly is associated with the Horned God's Holly King aspect. Holly is good for luck, marriage, dream magic, and masculinity. Planted around the house, Holly gives powerful protection. It is also often used as a Yule-time decoration.

- Lilac

Lilac is good for memory, luck, and wisdom. Lilacs can be either burned or crushed and placed in pillows or mojo bags.

- Mistletoe

Mistletoe is used for protection from negative energy, black magic, and other spells. It is also used for creativity and for protection against misfortune and ill health. It can be used to attract customers, advance employment and business goals, and attracting money. It can be worn in an amulet, placed in a mojo bag, or hung in the house.

- Oak

Like Holly, oak is associated with the Horned God, specifically the Oak King aspect. It is considered the most important and prominent of the kinds of trees. The leaves are useful if burnt to purify places and objects. The oak tree is the source of powerful wood for magical items such as wands and wooden statues for shrines. Oak is also worn as an amulet for fertility.

- Poppy

Poppy, also called opium poppy is good for abundance, prosperity, fertility, and love. It is useful to add poppy or carried in a mojo bag.

- Rosemary

Rosemary has a variety of uses including love and lust spells; clarity of mind and memory; removing negative energy and it is also used in purification rituals. It should be worn as an amulet while reading or studying, and it is burned, sometimes with other herbs, for protection. It can also be added to a pillow in order to prevent bad dreams.

- Sandalwood

Sandalwood is good for protection, exorcism, healing, and wish spells. It is also great for healing wands. Practitioners can write a wish on a chip and burn it in a cauldron while concentrating on the wish to make it a reality. Sandalwood is also useful for meditation and astral travel. Finally, it is good for improving energy and facilitating healing by aligning the chakras.

- Sunflower

Sunflowers increase power, wisdom, and energy. It is also useful in wishes. The sunflower was used as a magical symbol in Allen Ginsberg's poem Sunflower Sutra. Reciting the poem-sutra is a powerful incantation.

- Thyme

Thyme is an herb that increases affection, good impression from other people, and it attracts loyalty. Hung in the house, it ensures good health, helps with banishment, and protection for everyone who lives in the home. It can also provide courage and strength. Thyme can be burnt, worn, placed in baths, or placed in a dream pillow to ward off nightmares.

- Violet

Violet is good for dreams and prophetic visions. It is also useful for increasing peace, protection from evil and increasing creativity. Violet can be placed on an altar or a shrine, carried in a mojo bag or made into a crown in order to bring calm dreams and cure headaches.

- Witch Hazel

Witch hazel is useful for increasing healing and love. Witch hazel is good for protection against evil and lunar magic. Witch hazel can be worn when a loved one has died in order to overcome the sadness. Otherwise, it can be placed on an altar or shrine.

Chapter 6: Wiccan Spells

Casting spells and practicing magic is at the core of witchcraft. It is important to read and learn spells in order to understand them. It is also important to learn how to make your own spells so that you can customize your rituals and practices for yourself. This chapter will cover the essentials of making your own spells, as well as a collection of spells that are ready to be used by any practitioner.

Book of Shadows

A witch's spellbook is called a Book of Shadows or a grimoire. Spellbooks are volumes that contain spells for easy access. Books of Shadows can be purchased either from a bookstore or online. Witches can also create their own Book of Shadows with a blank book. A Books of Shadow does not just contain spells but also details of a coven's rituals and ceremonies.

How to Create Your Own Spells

Why create your own spells? It can be daunting to do so. Perhaps you lack confidence or are unsure that you are skilled enough to create spells. Don't worry. Below is a simple process that will help shape your spells so that you can embrace your spiritual creativity. Taking ownership of your practice is the key to becoming the greatest Wiccan you can be.

The first step in creating your spells is to define what they are and what you want to happen. It is very difficult for the divine and the elements to grant you what you want if they are unclear about that is. Spells should have a clear intent. If the spell involves other people, it is important to take them into consideration, especially if you know who those people are. After all, their energy and auras will surely affect the spell. Once you have a clear idea of what you want to happen, the next step is to gather the materials or resources you need.

It is important to have the correct materials when creating new spells. This can include known spell correspondences such as which day of the week corresponds to which type of spell as well as the magical tools one might use (see Chapter 5). One can choose a tool or tools based on the elements associated with the spell.

The next step is to find the words or incantations involved in the ceremony. What words will invoke power from the spirits or lend their selves to the healing ritual? While words in spells are not required, using them can help focus your magical energy. You can use a basic chant; many are available online, or you can create your own. The words of the spell might be a poem, with rhyming lines and other poetic devices. You can even use song lyrics that you have a deep and personal connection to; though those should be used sparingly as they are not as potent as words the practitioner comes up with.

Finally, it comes time to cast the spell. It is possible to go through all the motions of a spell, from reciting the words or making gestures, and still not be actually casting the spell. Casting the spell involves not only the process of the spell, but also the energy the practitioner can summon, visualize, and control. That energy has as much to do with the outcome as the magical tools, words, and gestures. It is also a good idea to meditate on the spell's outcome before attempting to spell.

Once a spell is created, it can be used or modified later. It is a good idea for the witch to record his or her spells in a book.

Different Types of Spells

There are several types of spells. The major types of magic are divination, high, low, elemental, sympathetic, talismanic, folk, and petition magic. Each form of magic has its own pros and cons.

- Divination

Divination is the art of seeing the future, be it an outcome or an event. There are several methods for divination. These methods are discussed in Chapter 5.

- High Magic

Despite its name, high magic is not better or worse than low magic. It simply indicates the amount of ritual and ceremony involved in the spell. High magic covens use a lot of specific words, gestures, movements, and tools in a very precise way in order to cast their spells. High magic is the most ritualized version of Wiccan magic, and it is especially prevalent in Gardnerian covens.

- Low Magic

Low magic is common earth and nature magic. Low magic is the magic that is minimally ritualized in contrast to high magic, where everything is ritualized. Low magic relies less on ceremony and more on inspiration, intuition, spontaneity, and creativity.

- Elemental Magic

Elemental magic deals with energy tied to the five elements of air, earth, fire, water, and aether. Elemental magic is raw and powerful, and its practice involves the precise association of the element with magical tools, chants, timing, and gestures. In elemental magic, it is important to include a strong symbol of the element such as a stone or crystal for the earth, a feather for air, a match for fire, or a cup or goblet of water or other magical concoction.

- Sympathetic Magic

Sympathetic magic is magic that uses an association between a person and an object. Through magic, the two become linked so that what happens to one happens to the other. While this process is often used in voodoo dolls and black magic, it is also useful to give the linked person healing, love, and positive energy.

- Talismanic Magic

Talismanic magic centers on the creation and wearing of a talisman or an amulet that is generally worn but can also be carried. Talismans are used to gather or repel certain types of energy, ward off an evil spirit and entities, or to act as a magical focus for other spells. Many magical tools are consecrated as talismans before they are used in ceremonies.

- Folk Magic

Folk magic is the common magic that is typically passed down from one generation to another. It is done around the home such as cleansing with a smoke stick. While folk magic is common, that does not mean it is less advanced or potent than other magics.

- Petition Magic

Petition Magic is where the witch makes a deal with an entity, spirit, or divinity. This spell is much like a contract, with the witch promising or giving something in return for the spirit's help. It is important to be clear about your intentions; spirits contacted through petition magic may have their own goals that might not coincide with the Wiccan practitioner.

Magical Tools

The major magical tools are the cup, pentacle, sword or knife, and wands. Each tool is associated with an element that also corresponds to a tarot suit. For instance, the cup is associated with water and the tarot suit of Cups. Another example is the knife, which is associated with fire and the tarot suit of

Swords. These major tools should appear in most spells, as they are the most powerful items in the witch's arsenal.

Other magical tools include besoms, cauldrons, censers, cingulum, jewelry, and smudge sticks. Besoms are brooms that practitioners jump over. Cauldrons are metal pots that are used to boil water, herbs, and other ingredients into a potion or to submerge objects for use in water spells. Censers are incense-holders that allow the smoke and scent to fill the area you are practicing in. The cingulum is cords worn at the waist. Cingula often indicate the initiate's rank in the coven, with different colors of cords representing different ranks. The jewelry and accessories the practitioner wears can change the spell on a deep level. Whether it is a pentacle necklace, an ouroboros ring, or a crown made of twigs and leaves, what we wear either empowers or dampens the spell. The energy of the item can have a drastic effect on the spell, and it is important to harness that untapped energy and put it to good use in a spell. Mojo bags are bags filled with herbs and stones that the practitioner carries with them. Finally, there is the smudge stick. Smudge sticks are bundles of herbs that are lit until they smoke. The smoke is a powerful tool for cleansing, especially for the place you live.

Even more mundane items such as candles, stones, lamps, and crystals can alter or empower the spell.

Before magical tools can be used they should be consecrated. The tools can be consecrated in a ritual conducted by the practitioner or their coven.

Spell Descriptions

Attraction

Attraction spells are powerful and designed to make the witch more attractive to possible mates as well as attracting positive energy.

Tools: The ritual will require a blank sheet of paper, a pen, and two candles.

Incantation: Bless me, oh Goddess, and bring forth that which I require!

Procedure: The Wiccan should meditate to clear her or his mind. Once the practitioner is calm, the desired result should be written on the paper. Next, light the candles and burn the piece of paper. To complete the spell take the ashes outside and let the wind take them.

Banishing

Banishing spells dispel curses, hexes, and black magic, or forces summoned supernatural beings to leave. This is especially useful if the summoned creature or spirit is evil like a devil, a demon, or a succubus.

Tools: A cauldron, a black candle, parchment paper, and a pen. Sometimes a wand is also used.

Incantation: Goddess of the Moon, banish this negativity from my home.

Procedure: First create a magic circle and build energy inside. Next, recite the incantation and write down the target of the banishment. Light the candle and let it burn down while the spell is being cast. Place the parchment into the boiling cauldron. If the practitioner is using a wand, trace the shape of a pentacle with it. Finally, open the circle and step outside. Once the candle has melted, dispel the circle.

Birthday Blessing

Birthday blessing spells are spells to bless the target on their birthday to bring the target good fortune and happiness not just on their birthday but also for the rest of the year.

Tools: A white candle

Incantation: Oh Goddess, oh god, bless this person on their birthday and let them have happiness and peace.

Procedure: Cast a magic circle and place the white candle in the middle. Light the candle and concentrate on the flame. Have the target of the spell make a wish and then blow the candle out. Open the circle an exit to complete the spell.

Cleansing

A cleansing spell is useful for consecrating magical tools, as well as removing hexes and black magic. Cleansing also removes negative energy.

Tools: Blessing oil.

Incantation: With sacred oil, I cleanse this home. May the Goddess and God bless this place, my home. Negative energy be gone!

Procedure: First the Wiccan should meditate to become calm. Next, clean the house and sweep the dirt outside the doorway. Once that is done, visualize a spider web being caught in the wind. Recite the incantation and sprinkle the oil in the doorways.

Confidence

A confidence spell helps with self-esteem, improving the practitioner's strength of character. This spell is useful in a romantic relationship, in work environments, and confidence in general.

Tools: A tiger's eye stone, a yellow or gold candle, and oil corresponding to the sun.

Incantation: I call upon the earth and the sun. Bring me self-worth and confidence.

Procedure: Draw a magic circle and sit in the middle cross-legged. Light the candle; place three drops of oil on it and tiger's eye crystal in the practitioner's cupped hands. Recite the incantation. Next, imagine yellow energy filling first the practitioner, then the circle, and finally the entire room. Once the room is filled, the practitioner should open their hands and allow the stone to absorb the magical energy. Let the candle burn out, and then open the circle. Carry the stone for greater confidence.

Counter spell

A counterspell is a spell that either dispels a curse, hex or counters negative energy. Counterspells are powerful protection from black witches and the practitioners of black magic. Whenever breaking a spell, there is a possibility that as the energy is released, it might cause damage to the witch, so the procedure must be done within a magic circle.

Tools: A candleholder, a black candle, and a cauldron.

Incantation: I call on fire. I call on water. I undo this spell. I break this spell. I am free. Blessed be the Goddess and God.

Procedure: Cast a magical circle with the cauldron in the middle. Place the candle inside and fill it to water until it is just under the wick. Light the candle and concentrate on visualizing the spell breaking. Recite the incantation and wait until the candle burns down to the water and is extinguished. Once done, open the circle and carry the candle outside. Bury the candle and sprinkle water over it.

Divination

As stated in Chapter 5, divination is the act of prophecy or learning an outcome of a future event. Below is a simple divination spell that allows the Wiccan to peer beyond time's veil.

Tools: A crystal ball or mirror, a small diamond, and a candle.

Incantation: Oh Goddess and God, open the doorway into the unseen. Open my eyes and bless me with prophecy.

Procedure: Cast a magic circle and place the crystal ball or mirror in the middle. Once the circle is cast, the practitioner should place the diamond in their hand. Recite the incantation and concentrate on the crystal ball or mirror until the unseen is revealed. Once completed, leave the circle.

Fertility

Fertility spells help to ensure not only that the woman is fertile enough to conceive, but also to increase masculine sexuality to avoid impotence.

- Female

Tools: A green candle and a sprig of basil.

Incantation: Oh Goddess, I beg for your blessing. Make my stomach swell with your power.

Procedure: Cast a magic circle and place the candle in the middle of it. Light the candle while reciting the incantation. Next, visualize pregnancy or a birth. Light the sprig and let it burn. Allow the candle to melt. When the spell is complete, open the circle and take the ashes of the basil outside and cast them into the wind.

- Male

Tools: A green candle and an offering for Cernunnos. The offering can include gains, fruit, acorns, and beer or wine.

Incantation: I summon thee! Oh, Cernunnos! Oh, Horned One! Come to this place of worship. In the wilderness I beseech you. Bring fertility to me in exchange for this offering.

Procedure: Go into the wilderness where civilization is distant such as a forest or a large park. Place the offering at the base of a tree and recite the incantation. Concentrate on the god and imagine a wave of energy going from the roots to the leaves of the tree. When the visualization is done, leave the offering at the base of the tree for Cernunnos to take at his convenience.

Note: When choosing the offering, make sure it is biodegradable.

Healing

As the name indicates, healing spells heal the target of the spell. This can mean healing physical ailments as well as mental or magical ailments. Healing spells require a lot of energy and require the spell to be closely tied to helpful herbs, crystals, and stones.

Tools: A strand of hair and a white candle.

Incantation: Goddess, may you heal this person. Let the pain and suffering subside.

Procedure: Cast a magic circle and light the white candle in the center. Take the hair sample of the person to be healed and burn it in the candle's flame while reciting the incantation. Next, visualize the healing needed and concentrate on it until the candle burns out. Once done, open the circle and leave it. Bury the candle outside.

House Protection

House protection spells are just what they sound like, spells that protect the home or a place of business. These words keep black witches, evil spirits, misfortune, and other ill effects from the place a Wiccan live, or by extension, the place the Wiccan works.

Tools: Fern leaves, a wand, and a smudge stick.

Incantation: Goddess and God close this barrier against [insert what you are trying to protect against such as evil spirits.]. Protect this place!

Procedure: Put dried up fern leaves on the ground in front of the doorways and on the windows. Take a smudge stick and let it burn at all entrances and exits. Next, draw a pentacle with the wand while reciting the incantation and concentrating on the protection by visualizing a wall of plants around the home.

Invisibility

This invisibility spell allows the target to go unnoticed unless she or he does something to bring attention to them. The spell does not literally make the target invisible but makes it so that people have a hard time noticing the target. The spell functions by placing an aura over the target that causes observers to ignore the target of the spell.

Tools: A small mirror.

Incantation: O, Mother Goddess, O, Father God, help your servant go unseen. Mask my movements from the eyes of others, make my tracks disappear.

Procedure: Cast a magic circle and place the mirror in the center. Sit down cross-legged and recite the incantation. Wait until the mirror appears dark and it turns upside down. Concentrate on being unseen. When the spell is concluded, open the circle and step outside. Place the mirror on an altar or shrine.

Love

Love spells improve the practitioner's physical attractiveness and increase desire in the target of the spell. Love spells help bind couples together and brings about unions that otherwise would not occur.

Tools: A red candle and a rose.

Incantation: Oh Goddess, bring on the love between two people. Take this rose and unite the lovers.

Procedure: Place the rose and candle on an altar or shrine. Light the candle and recite the incantation. Say the names of the targets of the spell. Concentrate on the candlelight and visualize the targets kissing. Allow the candle to melt until it is extinguished.

Money

As the name indicates, money spells are designed to bring wealth and money to the practitioner.

Tools: A penny, some clover, five green candles, and a cauldron.

Incantation: Oh Horned God, hear my call. Grace me with good fortune.

Procedure: Cast a magic circle and place a green candle at each point of a pentacle. Light the candles and place the cauldron in the middle of the circle. Recite the incantation as you place the coin and clover in the cauldron. Pour water into the cauldron and visualize money in your wallet or purse. Once the ceremony is over take the coin outside and bury it.

Remove Hate

Removing hate spells are very important for the Wiccan practitioner. They help in maintaining the Wiccan Rede.

Tools: A clear quartz crystal and incense.

Incantation: Goddess and God, I call on thee. Remove this hate in my heart. Cleanse me with your golden light.

Procedure: Cast a magic circle and place the quartz crystal in the middle of the circle. Light the incense and sit in meditation. While meditating, visualize white light that starts at the Wiccan's feet and moves up to the crown chakra. Once the energy reaches the chakra the practitioner should open the circle and step outside.

Sleep

Sleep spells are used to make sure that the Wiccan gets plenty of sleep and that it is a sound sleep. This spell can also be used to create a dream-like state for lucid dreaming.

Tools: A sapphire and a dream pillow.

Incantation: Oh, Goddess and God, bring sleep to my eyes and dreams to fill my mind.

Procedure: Place the sapphire beneath the dream pillow. Visualize the target sleeping while reciting the incantation. When the incantation is complete, have the target sleep on top of the dream pillow. The target will have pleasant dreams.

Stop Drinking

As the name suggests, the stop-drinking spell helps the target to stop drinking alcohol. The stop-drinking spell is a type of banishing spell, and it can also be used for any form of addiction.

Tools: An empty bottle of favorite alcohol, a glass of water, a pen, and a piece of parchment paper.

Incantation: Oh, Horned God! Oh, Goddess of the Moon! Come forth into my mind and heal my heart of this addiction. Rip it from my chest and allow me to breathe.

Procedure: Cast a magic circle and place the empty bottle in the center. Write the name of the addiction and the incantation on the parchment paper and place it inside the bottle. Recite the incantation and pour the water into the bottle. Concentrate on the addiction and when the spell is complete, open the circle and take the bottle outside and bury it.

Truth

Truth spells, as the name implies, are spells cast to learn the truth of a matter, no matter if it is a lie or a falsehood of some other nature.

Tools: An agate and a cauldron.

Incantation: Lords of Water, hear my call. Bring forth the truth to my eyes and ears. Blessed be at the Goddess and God.

Procedure: Cast a magic circle and place the cauldron in the middle. Place the agate in the cauldron. Pour water into the cauldron and recite the incantation. Concentrate on the truth you are seeking. Visualize a flower opening and the truth lies within. Take the truth from the flower. Open the circle and leave to complete the spell. Carry the agate to ensure truthfulness.

Elementalism Spell Correspondences

At its core, Wicca is an Earth or nature-based religion and the five elements are central to the practice of the craft. The five classical elements are air, earth, fire, water, and aether. Aether is the element that unifies the other four. Each element corresponds to specific rituals, magic, and symbolism in association with various other tools. For instance, each suit in the tarot deck is associated with an element, a direction or quarter, and other aspects of the element.

While the archangels are listed and seem to correspond to angels from Abrahamic religions, they are not specific figures in Wicca. Instead, they are metaphors derived from the divine Moon Goddess and the Horned God.

The directions of the elements are based on the geography of England where Wicca was first developed. The corresponding directions may be different based on the geographical area that a practitioner is in. For instance, someone on the East coast of the United States may use east as the element for water due to the Atlantic Ocean is to the East. Hence, the listed directions are suggestions but not set in stone.

Below are the elements and the aspects associated with them:

Element: Air

Symbol: A yellow triangle with a horizontal line through the middle

Gender: Masculine

Tarot Suit: Wands

Direction: East

Placement on Pentagram: Upper left

Season: Spring

Spirits: Zephyrs and fairies of air, wind, and flowers

Associated Animals: Eagle and ravens

Associated Symbols: Clouds, smoke, vapor, breeze, sky, and wind

Type of Magic: Divination, prophecy, wind magic, and concentration

Tools: Censer, sword, and wand

Element: Earth

Symbol: A green upside down triangle with a horizontal line through it

Gender: Feminine

Tarot Suit: Pentacles

Direction: North

Placement on Pentagram: Lower left

Season: Winter

Spirits: Dwarves, gnomes, and trolls

Associated Animals: Bull, cow, horse, and wolf

Associated Symbols: Caves, rocks, soil, and salt

Type of Magic: Binding, gemstone divination, runes, and prosperity (money)

Tools: Pentacle, pentagram, salt, stones, and gems

Element: Fire

Symbol: A red triangle

Gender: Masculine

Tarot Suit: Swords

Direction: South

Placement on Pentagram: Lower right

Season: Summer

Spirits: Firedrakes and salamanders

Associated Animals: Dragon, cat, snake, mantis, and Phoenix

Associated Symbols: Flame, lava, lightning, hot objects (specifically the stones), and volcanoes

Type of Magic: Healing, candle, love spells, and energy work

Tools: Candles, dagger, lamp, incense, herb burning, and paper requests.

Element: Water

Symbol: A blue upside down triangle

Gender: Feminine

Tarot Suit: Cups

Direction: West

Placement on Pentagram: Upper right

Season: Autumn

Spirits: Nymphs, mermaids, fairies of ponds, lakes, and streams

Associated Animals: Dragons, dolphins, frogs, and swans

Associated Symbols: Cups, rivers, lakes, ponds, rain, and fog

Type of Magic: Cleansing, protection, mirror magic, and lucid dreaming

Tools: Cauldron, cup, and mirror

Element: Aether (also known as Spirit)

Symbol: A circle or a wheel

Tarot Suit: Major Arcana

Direction: Universal

Placement on Pentagram: Upper

Season: The wheel of the year

Spirits: Sphinx

Associated Animals: Dove

Associated Symbols: None

Type of Magic: Spirit magic

Tools: Lamp

Conclusion

Thank you for making it through to the end of Wicca: Wiccan Spells for the White Witch. Let's hope it was informative and able to provide you with all of the tools you need to achieve your goals whatever they may be. Next, take the information from this book and explore Wicca for yourself.

The next step is to put this book down and begin practicing the craft. No matter if you are already a Wiccan or just interested in the subject, you can take the information from this book and take it to the next step. For many, it means beginning to practice witchcraft and the Wiccan religion.

If you feel overwhelmed, don't worry. Wicca is a broad subject with many fascinating aspects, but learning about it can be a daunting and it may require patience and perhaps a touch of creativity as you delve deeper into the mysteries of Wicca. To help keep from getting overwhelmed, it is important to purchase a blank book or use a word processor to create your own Book of Shadows.

It will be easier to understand Wicca if it is absorbed over time. The craft is a complex religion, but taking it in small parts and setting deadlines will help you learn it at your own speed. This is vitally important as many new Wiccans are too eager to skip to the magic and not ingest the rest of the book as they need to. Setting realistic goals will help the reader to fully comprehend the subject.

Once you have finished your initial preparations, note that they are just that, preparation. The next step is to take it to the next level and to begin worshiping the Goddess and God, practicing magic and performing rituals and ceremonies.

www.ingramcontent.com/pod-product-compliance
Lightning Source LLC
Chambersburg PA
CBHW020544080526
44583CB00013B/983